DATE DUE

DIGITAL PRIVACY
SECURING YOUR DATA

TAMRA B. ORR

Rosen
YA™
New York

Published in 2019 by The Rosen Publishing Group, Inc.
29 East 21st Street, New York, NY 10010

Copyright © 2019 by The Rosen Publishing Group, Inc.

First Edition

Names: Orr, Tamra B.
Title: Digital privacy: securing your data / Tamra B. Orr.
Description: First edition. | New York: Rosen Publishing, 2019 | Series: Digital citizenship and you | Includes bibliographical references and index. | Audience: Grades 7–12.
Identifiers: ISBN 9781508184638 (library bound) | ISBN 9781508184621 (pbk.)
Subjects: LCSH: Internet and children—Juvenile literature. | Internet—Safety measures—Juvenile literature. | Privacy, Right of—Juvenile literature. | Online social networks—Safety measures—Juvenile literature.
Classification: LCC HQ784.I58 O76 2019 | DDC 004.67'8083—dc23

Manufactured in the United States of America

CONTENTS

INTRODUCTION..4

CHAPTER ONE
KEEPING IT PRIVATE 7

CHAPTER TWO
SELECTIVE SHARING...19

CHAPTER THREE
GOOGLE YOURSELF 29

CHAPTER FOUR
IS THAT REALLY YOU? 41

CHAPTER FIVE
SECURE THAT DATA! 53

ACTIVITIES 64
GLOSSARY 67
FOR MORE INFORMATION...69
FOR FURTHER READING..72
BIBLIOGRAPHY...73
INDEX 76

INTRODUCTION

I magine getting an acceptance letter from a great college or university that you have been dying to attend. Or, picture landing that dream job. Now imagine all your good fortune was wiped out in an instant, not due to anything you did in the "real world" but due to an ill-considered post on social media or a comment on YouTube or a news website. Nowadays, one hears stories almost daily about how somebody damaged his or her career or future due to online activity. Whether someone embarrases himself or herself publicly in real time or in very old posts that are discovered and that reflect badly on him or her, internet activities can be hazardous to one's reputation if one is careless.

In today's world, it is so incredibly easy to share information online that you may think little about it. Going online is as much a part of your day as going to school, doing your homework, and watching television. A recent study done by Pew Research Center and the Berkman Center for Internet Society reported that:

- 91 percent of teens post pictures of themselves;
- 71 percent post their school name;
- 53 percent post their email addresses; and
- 20 percent post their cell phone numbers.

Taking precautions when you are online can feel a lot like flossing: you know it is good for you and you

Going online is a great way to do many things, like pay bills, do research, and especially to connect with friends. It can also come with unseen pitfalls, like compromising one's privacy.

should do it, but it often just feels like too much effort. Not taking precautions online can bring you a whole different set of troubles than a cavity or two might. If you do not keep your information private, it can (and most likely will) be used against you in some way. It might result in losing a job or a promotion, but it might also result in someone stealing your identity and taking your money (and, indirectly, damaging your credit score today and in the future). It can mean not getting into the college you wanted to attend the most or not getting a college loan. The potential pitfalls are many.

Social networking is wonderful—but part of what makes it so much fun to use is what also makes it dangerous. When you post anything on social media, just remember four very important factors:

- It is searchable—it can be found by anyone at any time.
- It is permanent—it does not go away even if you cannot see it and can be found now, next week, or in a decade.
- It is reusable—once someone finds your post, that person can copy it, share it, or even change it.
- It is invisible—you don't know where your information is going after you share it with your friends or what they decide to do with it.

Maintaining digital privacy exists to protect you and others you know. In this resource, you'll find out why you need it, how to get it, and what to do if you run into problems with it.

CHAPTER ONE

KEEPING IT PRIVATE

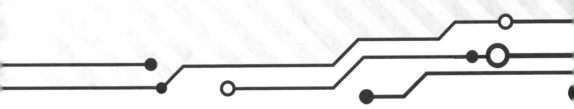

Nicole Orr is a digital nomad, the term used for someone who does a variety of online jobs from wherever he or she happens to be at the moment. For Orr, it has included writing a book review in a café in Bali, a blog post from a farm in Australia, and a story for a children's magazine from a coffee shop in Iceland.

Being a digital nomad means she gets to earn money while she travels. It also means that being extra careful online is essential. She states in an interview with the author:

> When it comes to digital security, nobody needs to be more careful than a digital nomad. If you saw one of us sitting in the corner of a café, you would likely notice the obvious stuff. There would be a laptop plugged into the wall, a cell phone sitting on the table, a backpack on the chair next to us, and a set of headphones around our necks. It's a common image, but it is also the image of digital danger. I know that when I am

Using free Wi-Fi in a public place is very convenient, but it can also open one up to having information and data scooped up by unsavory actors.

sitting in a coffee shop with my headphones on and my nose deep in a project, I am not really paying attention to anything other than my laptop. It is just too easy for someone to walk by my table, pocket my phone or tablet, and move on while I'm still just type-type-typing.

Digital nomads like Orr rely so completely on their electronic devices that they simply cannot risk anyone stealing them, or the information stored on them. Some of them use special apps and programs to protect their devices, while others just make sure to keep their

DATA PRIVACY DAY AND THE NATIONAL CYBER SECURITY ALLIANCE

Keep January 28 open on your calendar and help your community celebrate Data Privacy Day. This day "aims to raise awareness of the importance of privacy and data protection as well as to unite privacy professionals worldwide in celebrating the first legally binding international treaty dealing with the protection of personal data, Convention 108, signed January 28, 1981." It is not only celebrated throughout the United States but also in Canada and twenty-seven other countries. It is officially sponsored by the National Cyber Security Alliance, whose goals year-round are to educate consumers and organizations how to keep their data private. Its primary theme each year is Respecting Privacy, Safeguarding Data, and Enabling Trust. Although most privacy professionals celebrate on this day by attending conferences and learning more about digital privacy and security, you might want to celebrate it by deleting any information you are not ready to share, taking steps to secure what you want to keep, and finding out how to keep yourself and your information safer online.

devices out of view of strangers in public, especially if they are expensive or newer.

"Chances are, as a digital nomad, you will rarely be working somewhere alone, so you have to take special precautions," explains Orr. If you are working near a

Logging off of your accounts and shutting down one's devices when they are not in use are two simple ways to help protect one's digital privacy.

window, Orr points out, "All a stranger needs to do is hover over your shoulder and get away with whatever information is on your screen." She always keeps a wall at her back when she is in public.

Such precautions may seem extreme, but the risks they face are not much different from what you face when you go online from your house. The risk of someone getting your information, using that information, and causing you problems—from just embarrassment at sharing details with strangers to stealing your identity—is genuine.

AN ELECTRONIC HIVE MIND

Christopher Grant works at the call center for a bank, but he has been a tech geek his entire life. He took computer repair classes, has built and maintained computers from scratch, and has been on social media since before even Facebook was popular. Part of his job is to "keep my ears open for any warning signs that a customer may have fallen victim to a scam, because often times, they are not even aware they have been duped," he states in an interview with the author. He helps bank customers know what to do if their identities have been stolen or their online information has been compromised. "The internet has created a sort of electronic hive mind," he adds, "so, for better or worse, we all influence each other by what we contribute to it. But, like any physical organism, the internet is susceptible to disease. As we wash our hands, so we clean our computers of viruses. Digital privacy is an all-encompassing, worldwide concern."

Grant is right about digital privacy. It is a major concern in today's world, from the rich CEO and her company all the way to you sitting in your room with your laptop. How can you make sure what you are putting online will not come back and cause you problems? There are a number of actions to take and many to avoid.

PERFECT PASSWORDS

Let's start with account passwords. Everyone knows that a name, birthday, address, or some configuration of 123ABC are all bad choices. Most sites require passwords to have a minimum number of characters, and many stipulate they include a mixture of uppercase and lowercase letters, numbers, and special characters. Experts suggest your password be ten or twelve characters long, instead of eight. Passwords should not

It is suggested that passwords be complicated enough to throw off hackers but simple enough that users can easily remember them when needed.

be based on personal information because that makes them much easier to figure out. Instead, come up with something you will remember, but be creative. Make it something that no one else would ever understand, but you do.

Never share your password with others, especially in a text or email. Friendships change and you do not want to regret tomorrow what you casually did today. Don't post it on paper next to your monitor, under your keyboard, or in your desk drawer. If you have to write it down, keep it somewhere no one would ever look—like your sock drawer or under your trash can.

Finally, change your password on a regular basis. The Cyberbullying Research Center advises teens to change at least once a year. "Pick a time of year that will remind you to make the switch," it states on its website. "Get in the habit of changing your passwords at the start of each school year, on your birthday, or on some other memorable date," it suggests. "Just make sure you don't let passwords get stale!" Also, remember to use different passwords for different devices and online accounts. Can this get overwhelming to track? Of course. In that case, use a password manager such as Dashlane, LastPass, or SplashID, or keep a list in a very secure place.

PROPER PRIVACY

Whenever you are using a social media site, make sure you have chosen the best privacy settings for it.

VERY REAL POSSIBILITIES

Thomas Meyer is a software engineer in the research and development department of a leading website security company. Even as a young kid, he was fascinated by how to hack video games. He has been involved in information technology and systems for more than a decade. He emphasizes, like most IT experts, that whatever you put on the internet is never *gone,* so you simply must protect it.

In an interview with the author, he said:

Your information should be private and not shared with anyone without your consent. Many companies will look up a potential applicant and go through what they have posted to social media. If you think this does not affect their hiring decisions, you would be sorely mistaken. An offhand comment from someone referencing a medical condition can be used in the future to deny you health insurance. This may sound very 1984 and Orwellian, but there are all very real possibilities with the abundance of information we are providing about ourselves to the world via social media.

Finally, he advises people that just because you have nothing to hide does not mean should make the information public. As he puts it, "How we deal with our digital information and what happens when it is shared with third parties will set a precedent that will be hard to change down the road."

Though you might want all of your Facebook friends or Twitter followers to see your latest tirade about your little brother, you may not want the whole world to read about it.

A number of websites, as well as social media sites themselves, offer instructions on how to choose the proper privacy settings. Most privacy settings are found in your browser's Tools menu. (Because they tend to change often, it is best to go to the website to do the process rather than follow any directions here.) Connect Safely has an excellent, albeit dated, chart (http://www.connectsafely.org/facebook-privacy-chart -for-teens) that shows good advice about what teens

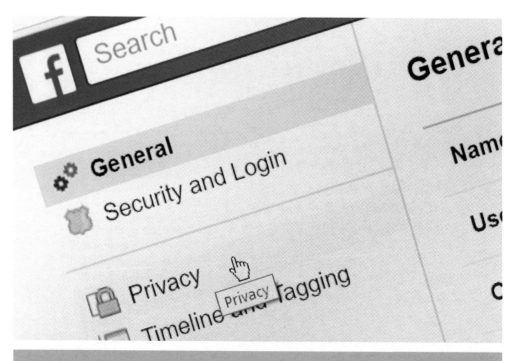

Any reputable site, such as Facebook, should have compre- hensive and easily accessible policies and measures covering privacy and security that help protect its users.

should share online and what settings are most recommended. For example, in contact information, the organization suggests that all teens leave the cell phone and address/city/town/zip code information blank. Your friends already know all of that information about you, and why would you want to share it with strangers anyway?

Speaking of friends ... do you really need hundreds of them? It is very easy to accept friend requests and followers on social media sites, but often you may do it casually, without really analyzing how, or even if, you really know this person. Limit your friends/followers to people you truly do know—at least in some aspect— and trust. Every few months, go through that list and eliminate anyone you do not recognize or simply have little connection with (either by "unfriending" or the less awkward "unfollowing").

UPDATE AND AUTHENTICATE

Two more steps that you can take to protect yourself online are update your security software and authenticate your URLs. Security software is essential for any computer, and it ranges from free to pretty decently priced. Some of the companies offering free antivirus software include Avast, AVG, Bitdefender, Kaspersky, and Avira. Keeping your security software up to date is vital since the malware it is protecting you from is always evolving.

Lastly, know what it means to have your emails authenticated. Basically, this protects you from a practice known as phishing, in which spammers try to trick you into giving them important private information for nefarious purposes—like stealing your money. Most email systems have an authentication program built into their Tools menu. If you are not sure how yours works, go online and search for "how to authenticate email on _____ network."

Michael Kaiser, executive director of the National Cyber Security Alliance, told *U.S. News and World Report* that using the internet safely is a lot like learning how to drive. He says, "You are going to learn how to drive as a young person and then you are going to drive for the rest of your life. It's going to be on you to do that as safely and securely as possible when you are out on the road—and the same can be true on the internet."

CHAPTER TWO

SELECTIVE SHARING

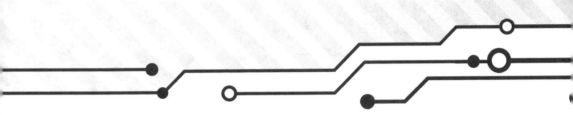

More than half a century ago, a song in a movie musical bemoaned, "Kids! What's the matter with kids today?" That statement has carried through countless generations, as older ones try to figure out the younger ones. This is certainly true today when parents try to figure out why teens are always online, what they are doing there, and what their activities might be revealing to unsavory actors. There is good news and bad news.

The good news is that, contrary to what many may think, most teens do not post online without giving it some thought first. "Teenagers aren't just posting carelessly," states Joanna Yau, lead author of a University of California, Irvine, study. "They're surprisingly thoughtful about what they choose to reveal on social media."

The bad news is that many posting decisions are based on whatever puts teens themselves in the best possible light (which is not always the wisest choice). "Peer approval is important during adolescence, especially in early adolescence," Yau continues, "so

Many selfies are perfectly acceptable ways of showing a friendly, positive face to the world, especially if you keep your pictures tame and acceptable for public consumption.

they're sharing content that they think others will find impressive." Only the pictures, posts, and captions that portray them the best will likely make it online. The question is then, what makes someone look good? Studying at the library or partying with friends? Spending time with family or goofing off at work?

Another study revealed that, of all of the information teens put online, they put more thought and effort in posting photographs of themselves. For most teens, the study reported, the picture has to look social, but not give away too much. It has to look good, but not draw too much attention. For many young people, selfies are fading fast. "The teens we interviewed were working hard, using multiple accounts, to create very carefully constructed versions of themselves for their friends and the outside world," reports Jane Tallim, coexecutive director of MediaSmarts. "At the same time, they were constrained by narrow social norms that discourage them being outside the mainstream, which was surprising as we tend to think of photo-sharing sites as venues for free expression and creativity."

SOBERING STATISTICS

Before you post another pic, comment, or tweet, take a moment to soak up some super sobering statistics:

According to the *New York Times*, 31 percent of college admissions officers visit an applicant's social networking page to learn more about the person. An article in *Time* also pointed out that 93 percent of potential employers view candidates' social profiles before making a hiring decision. What you post right now might well be viewed by either the person deciding whether to accept you at your first choice of colleges, or by the person who may decide whether you get that job you've been hoping to get. "Tools such as Facebook and Twitter enable employers to get a glimpse of who candidates are outside the confines of a résumé or cover letter," says Rosemary Haefner, chief human resources officer for CareerBuilder. "And with more and more people using social media, it's not unusual to see the usage for recruitment to grow as well."

What are the biggest red flags someone can post that would turn others against him or her? Controversial topics are number one. Clearly, drug and alcohol

THE WWGS RULE

Waffling on what to actually post or not post on your social media account? There is one relatively easy way to find out. Ask yourself a simple "WWGS" or "What would Grandma say?" If your grandma saw that picture you just posted, or that comment, or that conversation, or that opinion, how would you feel? If you think you would be embarrassed, think about why. It might be that your grandma is just really strict in what she thinks is right or wrong and you have very different values, or it could be a message to you that perhaps this is not the best thing to post.

Don't take this generic suggestion too far, though. You might want to post something about issues that Grandma might not necessarily buy into or fully understand—from bullying problems to venting about LGBTQ topics. In that case, go ahead and click to make sure to filter her out and other parties who you might not want to see that particular post. Just use the WWGS rule as a guideline, not a law.

Grandparents are often interested in the lives of their grandchildren, who should try to keep the content they see relatively wholesome.

abuse are near the top of the list. Sexual posts will certainly count against a poster, as will posts that verge into profanity, harassment, or a violent disposition. Discriminatory comments related to race, gender, or religion are strong negatives.

In addition, complaining about a job, fellow employees, or boss can hurt someone, even if you do not include any names in your posts. So can criticizing or making fun of clients or customers. In addition, according to Liz Soltan at the Digital Responsibility organization, "You may not realize it, but it's also a bad idea to share your religious beliefs, political views, or health problems publicly online, because that information makes you vulnerable to discrimination from current or future employers."

But it does not stop there. For 66 percent of hiring managers, poor spelling and grammar are going to count against a candidate, according to recruiting firm Jobvite. And, as Joseph Terach, founder and CEO of Resume Deli, puts it, "Your résumé and cover letter can show off your written communication skills, but not nearly as effectively as can your LinkedIn profile summary and Facebook posts. Think of these as portfolio pieces that your future employers will evaluate for both content and tone."

What counts in someone's favor? Volunteering time looks good, and recruiters also look for anything that indicates professional experience and examples of previous work. They look for creativity and originality, but also to see if someone would be a good fit with their business, their teams/employees, and their products. If

For prospective employers and schools, uncovering innocent and fun posts by searching someone's name is far better than finding compromising or controversial ones.

you want to keep your options open, you don't have to be a perfect angel, but the next time you want to post a comment or a picture, imagine your (future or theoretical) boss seeing it. You might change your mind.

AN INTERNET GHOST?

In case you are thinking you just need to completely stay off social media entirely, think again. More than half

VENT PATROL

Is there any time in the world that you want to post more than when you're really emotional? Whether someone fails a test, ends a friendship or relationship, or even wins a scholarship or lands a job interview, one impulse he or she may have is to go online to tell everyone. Venting online if you're angry or upset can be tricky, however. Since you are not face to face with whomever or whatever is upsetting you, it's easy to say too much or make inflammatory statements you would never make in person. A study published in the *Wall Street Journal* in 2015 pointed out that, surprisingly, venting does not really help people feel better. According to that research, venting actually makes them worse because they dwell on the issue and often get back responses that further upset them.

What should someone do instead? Try writing about your feelings in a journal or notebook, on paper. Call a good friend or family member and share your news. Go for a walk, run, or bike ride; kick a ball around; or even meditate. If these options don't work for you, check online for safe websites where you can vent completely anonymously. One site, Muttr, offers the chance to complain without being identified. Other options are Yik Yak, Vent, Whisper, or Secret. According to its website, Vent's goal is to allow you to "voice your opinion to our supportive community without the worry of being insulted or disrespected, de-friended, or upsetting people you know." You can categorize your post under a specific type of emotion, such as "furious," for example. Such sites allow users to share their opinions and thoughts without identifying themselves. However, these sites come and go quickly, so do your research and make sure they are still operating.

Writing things down in a notebook can be a great form of self-care that doesn't overly jeopardize one's privacy.

of all employers are less likely to pursue an applicant if they cannot find anything online at all about the person. They want to find information—but information that tells them they are making the right choice in picking you. As Joseph Terach told Careerbuilder.com, "Your social media profiles should be seen as an opportunity to shine—not a minefield."

There are ways to make social media work for you. CareerBuilder advises young people to keep their social media profiles updated. If you have a professional site, be sure to add recent skills and use keywords that make you searchable. In addition, follow your ideal employer's or college's social media accounts. This helps you keep up to date on what is happening there and if you would be a good fit.

Social media is fun. It can also be an effective tool, if used properly. Terach emphasizes that young people can still go online and be themselves, but it must be done carefully. He adds:

> You can be direct, opinionated and even a little brash. What you want to avoid is the extreme cases of these, i.e., don't be unreasonable, offensive and/or closed-minded. Again, being able to toe that line is the difference between sharing content that affects readers' opinions and thoughts, and just "mouthing off" on social media.

CHAPTER THREE

GOOGLE YOURSELF

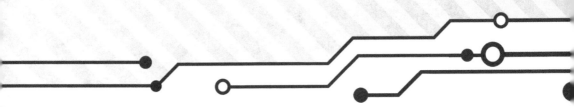

You use it every day. It answers almost every question you can come up with and offers details you are not sure you even wanted to know. No other search engine is used as often as Google is. (Google is number one in 2018, followed by Apple Safari, Firefox, and Internet Explorer.) Chances are that Google knows way more about you than you do about it. In fact, according to research, here is what Google knows about almost all people who are online and using it as their browser:

- If they have the location tracking turned on their phones (and most people do), Google knows where they have been. Not just where, but when, and how long it took them to get there.
- It knows every single thing users have gone online to search—on any of their devices.
- It knows, via profiles, people's location, gender, age, hobbies, job, interests, relationship status, and income.

- It knows what apps users use, how often they use them, where they use them, and with whom they use them.
- It records users' YouTube history. By tracking the videos users watch or browse, Google (YouTube's owner, with both companies now part of Alphabet, Inc.) can figure out if they are traveling, need extra help in calculus, are trying to lose weight, or are obsessed with Korean pop music.
- It knows which events users attend (from concerts to job interviews) and when.
- If they use Google email, it has every single email sent and received.
- It has every image users searched for and saved, every article

Google, and its parent company, Alphabet, Inc., offer many interconnected platforms. These services track a great deal of private information and content about their users.

they have looked up and read, and every ad they ever clicked.

Google provides a user option of providing all of the information it has on anyone in print form. Users opting for this record should be prepared, because it can even run into millions of pages. As data consultant and web developer Dylan Curran reports in *The Guardian:*

> This link includes your bookmarks, emails, contacts, your Google Drive files, all of the above information, your YouTube videos, the photos you've taken on your phone, the businesses you've bought from, the products you've bought through Google ... They also have data from your calendar, your Google hangout sessions, your location history, the music you listen to, the Google books you've purchased, the Google groups you're in, the websites you've created, the phones you've owned, the pages you've shared, how many steps you walk in a day.

What about Facebook? The amount of information Facebook collects about its user accounts is just as staggering. It includes every message ever sent or received; every log-in, with time and duration; and all the applications a profile has enabled and used. Curran adds:

> The data they collect includes tracking where you are, what applications you have installed, when you use them, what you use them for, access to your webcam and microphone at any

time, your contacts, your emails, your calendar, your call history, the messages you send and receive, the files you download, the games you play, your photos and videos, your music, your search history, your browsing history, or even what radio stations you listen to. This information has millions of nefarious uses. You say you're not a terrorist. Then how come you were googling Isis? Work at Google and you're suspicious of your wife? Perfect, just look up her location and search history for the last ten years. Manage to gain access to someone's Google account? Perfect, you have a chronological diary of everything that person has done for the last ten years. This is one of the craziest things about the modern age.

Curran points out that we would never allow the government or corporations to put surveillance equipment in our homes, but that peole are far more lax about letting their phones be surveiled.

MEET YOUR ONLINE PROFILE

Do you have any idea of what your online profile is like? If you don't, you're not alone. Many people have no idea. How can they find out? They can start by doing a search on themselves—and not just once, but regularly. If they are serious about it, people should be as fastidious with their online presence as they are with their financial and credit histories. Before they start, however, experts

A STUMBLE FOR FACEBOOK

When Facebook founder Mark Zuckerberg had to sit in front of Congress and explain how he had allowed a data collection agency to collect information on millions of its users, it was a wake-up moment for many internet users. People knew that Facebook gathered information on its users. That is why the ads targeted users' very specific browsing habits and posts.

But few knew that facts were also being acquired by a company known as Cambridge Analytica in order to potentially sway the 2016 presidential election. Zuckerberg claimed to be surprised, too. In a phone call with members of the press on April 4, 2018, he stated:

> We didn't focus enough on preventing abuse and thinking through how people could use these tools to do harm as well. That goes for fake news, foreign interference in elections, hate speech, in addition to developers and data privacy. We didn't take a broad enough view of what our responsibility is, and that was a huge mistake. It was my mistake.

> Facebook says it has taken a number of steps in order to make sure this kind of data theft never happens again.

recommend that they be sure to use a browser while not logged in to any of their user accounts, especially Gmail, Google, or other ones that track their activity. Otherwise, Google and other browsers will personalize the results you get, based on your account activity.

Put your name in the search box and see what comes up. Be sure to use all permutations of your name—full name (for example, Samantha Louise Collins), name with initials (Samantha L. Collins or S. L. Collins), your proper first name (Samantha), along with your shortened names (Sam, Sammy). Don't stop at Google though. Check out Bing, Yahoo, and DuckDuckGo, just in case. Also, after typing your name, add the word "photos" and see what comes up. What photographs come up? Do you recognize all of them? Do you want all of them easily accessible online?

If you made the winning goal during your school's soccer championship, it is possible that your school's or local newspaper's story on it may feature both your name and image.

Besides photographs, are there any articles about you? There could easily be—perhaps you made the winning free throw in a basketball game and a sports reporter described it. Maybe you won a scholarship, got first place in a contest, or did any one of a million other things that could land your name in a local newspaper, newsletter, or magazine. You might regularly comment on blogs and use your name, or you might generate your own content online. All of these things can show up in a search.

TAKING IT DOWN

When internet users encounter something they do not like—from unflattering photos to negative coverage about them on a blog or news site, it is awfully tempting to reach out and leave a nasty comment or argue with what has been said. Ignore that temptation. Usually, that will only make things worse. Recent activity will make that photo or article easier and faster to find, and now people have something to reply to, and may not respond very nicely. Google and other search engines have specific processes for removing pages or posts, but there are limits on what they are willing to take down. For example, Google is usually willing to help users wipe clean sensitive information like financial data or identification numbers.

According to the Digital Millennium Copyright Act (DCMA), in many cases, it is actually illegal for someone

Just as posting other people's artwork online for profit can be complicated and even illegal, posting images of private individuals without their explicit permission is just as tricky.

to post a picture of you online without your permission. If you find such a photo, based on the DMCA, you can tell him or her to remove the photo. If the website doesn't comply, you would have grounds to sue for infringement.

DIGITAL PRIVACY AND CYBERBULLYING

What do staying private online and cyberbullying have in common? When people post information about themselves online, it can raise their risk of being harassed or bullied. More than half of all teens have reported being cyberbullied at some point. According to the *Patriot-Ledger*, 40 percent say it has happened more than once, and 20 percent say it happens once or twice a month. Almost a quarter of teens say that the number-one reason they check their social media is to make sure no one is saying mean things about them! Amazingly, 95 percent of teens who have seen bullying happen online have chosen to ignore it, largely because they have no idea what to say or how to respond.

What kind of bullying is done online? Some examples include the following:

- Excluding others intentionally from an online group.
- Cyberstalking by sending emails, messages, or tags that others do not want.
- Gossiping in ways that damage reputations or relationships.
- Tricking others into revealing secrets and then sharing them online.
- Sending offensive, insulting, or cruel messages repeatedly.
- Threatening some kind of violence.
- Posting online arguments and offensive comments, or flaming, on websites, forums, or blogs.
- Impersonating someone by creating fake accounts and then posting messages designed to embarrass the person or damage a reputation or relationship.

According to the Megan Meier Foundation, about 13 percent of students who have been cyberbullied do not want to go to school the next day. That may not sound like many, but that comes to 6.7 million kids—equal to just under the entire population of Tennessee. Even worse, bullied youth are more likely to attempt suicide than those who do not experience bullying. When schools, parents, and communities do not take cyberbullying seriously—or not as seriously as bullying in person—they are overlooking a clear and present danger to young people.

Avoid posting information or content that attracts these bullies. If you see harassment happen online, don't let the bullies get away with it. Don't participate in it or ignore it when you see it happening. Speak out, speak up, and perhaps you will save someone's life. Even if someone fears getting involved and attracting negative attention from bullies, he or she can report suspicious or hostile activity anonymously, and contact webmasters, moderators, or other responsible parties. They might even need to involve enforcement officials if the activity has shifted into criminal abuse.

There is good news and bad news about trying to remove content or posts online. The bad news is that it is never actually, completely, totally gone. As the experts at Reputation Management put it, "Throughout your removal process, keep in mind that the Internet, in many ways, 'never forgets.'" If the information was there once, it still is—but now

The Wayback Machine, run by a nonprofit organization called the Internet Archive, allows users to look up posts from long ago as well as deleted posts and content.

it is archived or cached by the search engine. So, what's the good news? It can take a very persistent searcher to find it, and most people are not interested enough to make that much effort.

Consider how much companies, the government, and other parties know about internet users. This makes carefully considering one's activities online all the more important. Otherwise, not only can you be faced with some serious problems or embarrassment but someone might just decide to take that information and steal it. Suddenly, the world has more than one of you!

CHAPTER FOUR

IS THAT REALLY YOU?

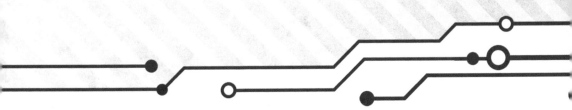

C aspian was shocked when he checked his online checking account. It had less than half of what he thought was in there. A quick look and he could see that someone had gone shopping online—but it certainly wasn't him. The person had ordered hundreds of dollars' worth of stuff. Caspian got immediately on the phone with his bank, talking to the fraud department. He discovered that although his experience was stressful, he was far from alone.

According to consulting firm Javelin Strategy, about one in sixteen people in the United States fall victim to identity theft each year. That is more than fifteen million Americans. Some, like Caspian, just find unfamiliar charges on their debit cards. Others do not find out for months that someone has used their information to open up credit card accounts and bank loans. Victims might be in the dark until their credit reports reveal unpaid bills and possibly even legal judgments against them. That can devastate a person's credit score, which

Privacy involves not only keeping one's reputation untarnished but also protecting one's financial data, bank and credit card accounts, and credit history.

can cripple his or her ability to apply for home and car loans, rent apartments, and engage in other economic activities.

"The criminals are getting better at committing this fraud," explains Al Pascual, research director and head of fraud and security at Javelin Strategy and Research. "They learn and they adapt and they find workarounds to the solutions we put in place." One of the types of fraud that jumped the most was identity thieves using stolen credit and debit card numbers to buy things online or over the phone.

"We think of stopping fraud like squeezing Jell-O—when you stop it one place, it squirts out someplace else," says Stephen Coggeshall, chief analytics and science officer at Lifelock. "These fraudsters are pretty smart and they continue to look for the weakest points of attack."

A rising threat in the identity theft arena is hijacking people's cell phone accounts. After getting your Social

A passcode on a phone is a good first defense against parties trying to compromise your privacy.

Security number, it is easy for criminals to hack into your account and grab your email and text messages. Why do they want to do this? Who cares about your Aunt Jeanine's email recipe for cinnamon rolls, or your

best friend's texted opinions about the school's new backpack policy? Of course, texts and emails sent to one's phone often have passwords and other sensitive information on them. Nowadays, many users' phones are linked to bank accounts, credit and debit cards, and payment processing apps like PayPal.

TOP 10 SAFETY RULES

There are lots of important safety rules in place when using the internet. Here are a few general ones, with some help from experts Thomas (IT expert) and Christopher (tech support worker for a major bank's call center):

• Do not use the same password on multiple sites. Thomas states, "Password cracking software has become incredibly good and if you reuse the same password for all of the sites you visit, the attackers will have access to all of your social media, bank accounts, etc." Remembering multiple passwords can feel overwhelming, so he recommends using a password manager, software designed to encrypt and store all of your passwords that is unlocked with a single master password.

- Only do business with companies you really trust. Christopher says to always check for a lock icon next to the address bar on your internet browser. "Set up a PayPal account or other online payment system to function as a secondary bank account," he suggests. "This allows you to make purchases indirectly, further protecting your account."

- Always have some kind of antivirus software protection on your computer. Most companies offer low yearly subscriptions, plus there are a number of free software options that offer base-level protection.

- Avoid sharing your computer with others you don't know and trust. If you have no choice, log out of all of your accounts when finished and do not display any information that is sensitive.

- Password protect all of your electronics. If you lose a portable device, there is no telling who may find and exploit it for his or her own purposes.

- Watch the news for any kind of security breaches. Keep an eye out for headlines regarding data security. Watch for anything that possibly pertains to you.

- If anyone contacts you requesting personal or financial information, hang up. Banks and other legitimate institutions will very rarely—if ever—contact you and request any information.

- Make a list of what is in your purse or wallet and leave the list somewhere safe at home. Update the list regularly as you add or remove important cards or data. (This way you will know if something is

If you are visiting a public place, it is important to remain mindful of one's possessions, including smartphones, since their theft can easily expose any user to multiple dangers.

missing right away.) Never carry your Social Security number, account PINs, or passwords in your wallet or purse, where they could be stolen or misplaced.

- Go digital with your banking. If you are paperless, you won't have to worry about mail getting lost or stolen. Check your account online often, scanning transactions to make sure nothing is suspicious.
- Never feel so secure about your security that you stop being vigilant. Some people can have their identities stolen more than once, even after they have reported the activity to the proper authorities.

FIGHTING BACK

Identity theft can happen to anyone, and part of the reason is internet users putting much personal information online. So, now what? Is there a solution or are you just doomed? Having your identity stolen isn't fun—but

YOU ARE THE PRODUCT

If you want to know more about cybersecurity, ask Leon R. His old job taught him a lot. "I used to break into banks to help them find and fix security vulnerabilities before hackers get to them," he explains in an interview with the author. "This is known as 'penetration testing.' If you look for weak points, but do not actually attack, it is called 'threat and vulnerability.'"

Leon says:

In a lot of ways, privacy is dead. There is so much data collected and algorithms have become so advanced, that unless you use extraordinary measures to protect your privacy, you almost don't have any. You have to take as many precautions as possible because you don't know who or how the data is being used. You would be shocked how many tracking beacons are on sites you visit. All gathering data on every single thing you do.

Currently Leon is in school for data science, where he is working on building new systems designed to help prevent hackers from penetrating vulnerable networks and servers. He spent fifteen years in the hacking business. He has four important pieces of advice for young people today. First, as he puts it, remember that "anything you put on the internet never, ever leaves. You think you're deleting your pics from Instagram?" he asks. "You are not. They stay on Facebook and Insta servers—you just don't see them anymore."

Second, Leon recommends you install tools like Ghostery and "run around the web to see how many beacons are on every single page. It's scary!" Third, he points out that no one knows how data about you might be used. "Imagine applying for a job and stupid snaps from when you were fourteen or sixteen, or anything that you did that got you in trouble, come back to haunt you." Finally, he adds, "Remember, if you are not charged for the product, you are the product. Simple but powerful. It means that the company makes money off your data."

it isn't the end of the world, either. Here are Bankrate's recommendations if it happens to you:

- Immediately get in touch with your bank and any creditors you might have. Don't wait to do this. Although the Fair Credit Billing Act limits your liability for unauthorized charges to $50, that is only if you report them within two business days. After that, the liability can go to $500.

- Call a major credit reporting agency and request a fraud alert. Notifying one of these companies means they will all get the information and stay in place for ninety days.

- If you have a credit report, check it. These reports are free, so check them thoroughly for any accounts you do not recognize, payment history you do not remember, employers you never worked for, etc.

- Fill out an ID theft complaint and affidavit from

the Federal Trade Commission (FTC). This will be your official theft report.
- Change every single account password. Make them each different and strong.

In April 2018, a group called Raging Grannies demonstrated in front of Facebook's Menlo Park, California, headquarters to demand better privacy policies and consumer protections.

- If someone misused your Social Security number, report it. Social Security has a fraud hotline just for this purpose.
- Get a new driver's license or find out if yours has been compromised. Someone has been using your ID and that may mean your driver's license number. You can do this at your local DMV.
- Contact your mobile phone provider. Let the company know what happened so that if someone tries to open an additional account under your name, the provider will not do it.

For further details and helpful information, the FTC offers more help on how to recover from identity theft, so visit its website for additional information.

Clearly, there are many risks to putting too much personal information online, and one of the biggest risks is that someone may come across it and decide you are what he or she is looking for: a mark for fraud. Protecting your privacy is vital in a world where your very identity can be stolen and used in ways that can have repercussions for years to come.

CHAPTER FIVE

SECURE THAT DATA!

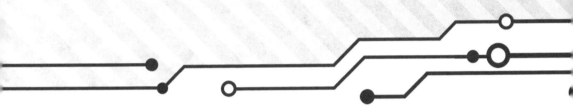

A man goes to his doctor and says, "My shoulder hurts very badly whenever I do this," and he waves his arm overhead wildly. The doctor frowns and writes something down on his notes. "I have just the cure," he says, handing the piece of paper to the patient. It reads, "Quit waving your arm over your head."

It is the same thing when it comes to digital privacy. If you don't want it to be stolen or misused, quit posting it. Unfortunately, you know that is pretty unlikely. Taking precautions is vital, but never posting anything remotely personal is unrealistic. Keep certain data as secure as possible while engaging as a digital citizen. Install and make use of antivirus software, employ strict authentication, and use a password manager if possible.

CHOOSE YOUR WEAPON

Look online and you can find endless advice on different ways to keep your online information safe. Much

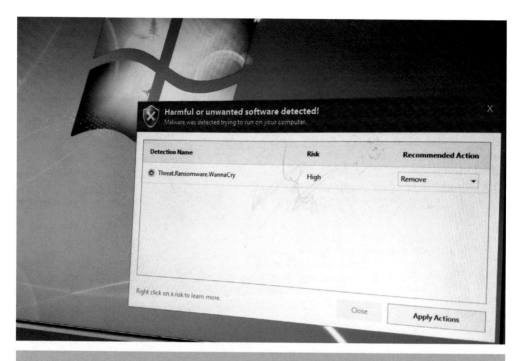

Harmful or unwanted software detected!
Malware was detected trying to run on your computer.

X

Detection Name	Risk	Recommended Action
Threat.Ransomware.WannaCry	High	Remove ▾

Right click on a risk to learn more.

Close   Apply Actions

Make sure to do a periodic scan for viruses and other breaches that could potentially result in someone stealing private information, content, and passwords from your computer or other device.

of it comes from companies trying to sell a product. Though having an antivirus installed on one's computer is important, internet users are well advised to do some research first on impartial, objective websites like *PC Mag* or *Consumer Reports*. They do extensive testing of antivirus software each year to determine the best choices for customers' money. Although antivirus software is primarily designed to protect users from any computer viruses, most of it does more than that. It is often these special features that help protect user data.

BIG BUSINESS BREACHES

If you follow the news, you might have heard how large companies, organizations, and even government agencies can also suffer digital privacy and security disasters. In 2017, the major credit reporting agency Equifax was hacked. As many as 143 million Americans, Canadians, and British consumers had their personal information compromised. The hacking took place for more than two months before Equifax became aware of it. Beth Givens, executive director of the Privacy Rights Clearinghouse, told the *Washington Post,* "The type of information that has been exposed is really sensitive. All in all, this has the potential to be a very harmful breach to those who are affected by it." Equifax was not alone. In 2013, when Yahoo was hacked, all three billion accounts were affected to one extent or another.

More recently, Mark Zuckerberg's Facebook ran into trouble when the personal data of as many as eighty-seven million users was obtained by a firm known as Cambridge Analytica. Facebook provided the information to a company for research purposes, but that company instead sold it to Cambridge Analytica, a firm closely tied to President Donald Trump's 2016 campaign. As Christopher says, "How much of the information was used—and to what end—is still not clear, and it is that uncertainty that worries me the most."

In *PC Mag's* 2018 review of antivirus software, it stated, "Among the other bonus features you'll find are secure browsers for financial transactions, secure deletion of sensitive files, wiping traces of computer and browsing history, credit monitoring, virtual keyboard to foil keyloggers, cross-platform protection, and more. You'll even find products that enhance their automatic malware protection with the expertise of human security technicians." The reviewers added, "We're seeing more and more antivirus products adding modules specifically designed for ransomware protection. Some work by preventing unauthorized changes to protected files. Others keep watch for suspicious behaviors that suggest malware. Some even aim to reverse the damage. Given the

In September 2017, it was revealed that private credit reporting agency Equifax had more than 145 million individual accounts breached by a hack.

growth of this scourge, any added protection is beneficial." Which companies made the top of the 2018 list? The top three were McAfee Antivirus Plus, Webroot SecureAnywhere Antivirus, and Symantec Norton Antivirus Basic.

Sent Mail

Drafts

Spam (42)

Drafts

Starred

Spam we receive might be both annoying and amusing, but it can also cause great harm to those who are fooled into opening strange emails or clicking dangerous links.

KEEPING IT AUTHENTIC

You know how you log in to some sites and have to answer those annoying security questions to prove it is really you? They may irritate you, but that authentication process really, truly is for your protection. For example, you don't want someone who stole your debit card to be able to log in and access your money just because he or she has your card. Instead, he or she must have your PIN, plus answer security questions like "What is your favorite beverage?" or "What was the name of the street you lived on as a baby?" Most authentication programs have at least one or two factors you must know, such as your account number, your pin, and a security question answer. Some have more than that—and though it is time-consuming, it is what helps protect you from someone else getting access to your accounts.

LISTENING TO MANAGEMENT

Remember when passwords were simple? This is no longer the case. The more complex you make them, the safer they are. Experts recommend you choose a phrase or mix of letters and numbers that is meaningless to everyone except you. Of course, trying to remember which bizarre phrase goes

EXPERT ADVICE

Leanne Coffman, head of the Safety Training Solution, started out minimizing physical risks and hazards in the workplace. Later, she moved on to digital security. "Over the years, we have shifted to providing assistance in digital privacy for virtually all of the firm's clients," she told the author. "I consider it vital for company health, because digital privacy, if not maintained properly, can damage a business reputation irrevocably." Coffman thinks young people, who might be future employees for these companies, should know the responsibilities that come with digital information. "While we live in a climate that is heavily invested in data and it's a wonderful aspect of modern life," she said, "there is also an equal responsibility to maintain personal information as confidential."

Coffman crafts policies for clients' phone usage, data protection, and defining and securely storing confidential information. Safety Training Solution also has programs installed to remotely wipe computers and cell phones if lost, and data policies in place for storage and use. Employees sign a data usage policy preventing them from identifying themselves as one of her employees on social media without express permission. That policy puts a layer between the firm and the employee in the case that the employee has a political or personal opinion that is controversial.

"We teach that harassment online is the same as personally harassing another and we have a no-tolerance policy for that, as well as a Duty to Report policy," Coffman adds. "Should another employee see such a discriminatory or threatening post by a coworker, they report it to our firm. In a small business, damage control is best done by prevention and we seek to prevent as much open data as possible."

with each site can be overwhelming. That is when password managers come in. A number of companies offer this service for a fee, such as LastPass or 1Password. With a manager, you create a master password and it gives you access to all of those individual passwords you have for different sites.

Another good piece of advice is to shut down any old accounts you are not using. Use password protection of some kind on your cell phone, whether it is high tech, such as fingerprint ID, facial recognition, or iris scanning, or simple, such as a pattern you draw or extra number you input. Don't make any purchases or send sensitive information when using public Wi-Fi.

An article in *The Guardian* points out that when Tim Berners-Lee first coined the term "World Wide Web," he probably meant an "organic linking of sites and pages." However, as time has passed and the internet has grown at light speed, author John Naughton has a different description in mind. He writes, "Imagine a

Cybersecurity has grown into an industry worth billions. Here, an attendee walks by a display at the 3rd European Cybersecurity Forum in Krakow, Poland, in October 2017.

CYBERSEC

**EUROPEAN
CYBERSECURITY FORUM**

ING WITH
R DISRUPTION

gigantic, global web in which are trapped upwards of two billion flies. Most of those unfortunate creatures don't know, yet, that they are trapped. After all, they wandered cheerfully, willingly, into the web. Some of them even imagine that they could escape if they wanted to. We are those insects," he continues. Technologists, developers, tech CEOs, journalists, and others who are involved with building the infrastructure, software, and apps of our online world all point out that all of us must now deal with the world we created. That means taking security and privacy seriously, even as so many factors contribute to compromise them.

ACTIVITIES

Activity 1
Search Yourselves

Form a small group with friends or fellow students to see just how much of your information is out there, using your own devices or ones provided at school. You can perform any or all of the following:

- Look up each group member by first and last name, within quotes. For example: "John Doe"
  - What hits did you get on the first few pages of the Google search?
  - Were there pictures included in group members' search results?
- Next, include the same information, but add your town's or city's name into the search, too. For example: "John Doe" Cincinnati, Ohio
- Add the names of schools, teams to which one belongs, churches, and other things with which group members are associated. Track how the results might change according to these elements.
- Use the original name searches, and add different social media sites into the search fields (Facebook, Instagram, Tumblr, etc.) to see what other kinds of hits appear.
- Discussion: Which, if any, of the results may be problematic or concerning for the subjects in question? Why?

Activity 2
In the News

Team up with three or more classmates to explore

how stories regarding privacy in the news have played out.

- Brainstorm any stories involving politicians, celebrities, and musical artists.
- Use the internet, including Google and other platforms, to find information, articles, and commentary on the respective stories/cases.
- Analyze how private information or content that damaged someone's reputation (or revealed him or her to be a wrongdoer), or explicit images, was revealed or exposed: accidentally, via the person's own mistakes or missteps; by law enforcement action, anonymous tip; intentionally and maliciously by an ex-partner, friend, or other party; or by any other means or sources that students might be able to identify.
- Create a chart that tracks visually the types of privacy breaches, how they occurred, and what the consequences were for victims, perpetrators, and even third parties.
- Discuss with fellow team members points of weakness in their own online personas, social media accounts, and online footprints. What might they learn from their own experiences, as compared to those of the aforementioned stories and scandals?

Activity 3
Privacy and You

1) Students in a group discuss what aspects of digital privacy most directly apply to their own experiences, and those of close friends, family members, and those in their community. Each student then picks a different aspect of privacy that appeals to him or her, or that he or she feels is important. For example:

- Measures to protect one's accounts on social media, including selective sharing of information to only select users, friends, and family
- Password protection, encryption, and other methods to protect financial information and records
- Carefully curating photos, including searching old posts and accounts to uncover potentially compromising ones
- Any other aspect of online privacy that students might brainstorm.

2) Students are each assigned a short presentation to develop that they will present to the others, or even in front of a classroom to a larger audience. They may use slides, video, and any other means to convey their findings and recommendations.

GLOSSARY

affidavit The written version of a sworn statement.

antivirus Software installed on a computer, laptop, or other device designed to combat viruses and other dangerous programs.

authenticate To confirm the truth of something.

breach A failure to maintain something, whether it is a contract or the security of a system.

chronological A way of tracking or looking at something from the earliest event to later ones.

credit score A number reflecting a person's credit history that helps others determine his or her likelihood of paying loans and settling other debts.

cyberstalking Harassing someone online in a way that makes him or her feel unsafe.

discriminatory Describes policies or actions that are prejudicial in a way that unfairly disadvantages one or more groups of people, or provides advantages or privileges to other groups.

flaming The act of intentionally upsetting or insult someone online.

hive mind A phenomenon in which many people think and behave the same way simultaneously.

inflammatory Describes something that is highly upsetting or offensive and liable to spark conflict.

infringement The act of encroaching on someone's rights or his or her creative or intellectual property.

keylogger A computer program that records every keystroke made by a user in order to gain access to data.

liability Something for which somebody is responsible, especially a debt.

lock icon A padlock symbol displayed in a web browser to indicate security.

malware Software or computer code that attackers can sneak into unsuspecting victims' computers or other devices, designed to damage, disable, or spy on them.

ransomware Malicious software designed to block access to a computer system until a sum of money is paid to the ransomer.

susceptible Vulnerable to something.

FOR MORE INFORMATION

AccessNow
PO Box 20429
Greeley Square Station
4 East 27th Street
New York, NY 10001
(888) 414-0100
Email: info@accessnow.org
Facebook and Twitter: @accessnow
AccessNow's mission is to defend and extend the dig-
  ital rights of users at risk around the world. It dedi-
  cates its mission to providing for open and secure
  communications for all.

Canadian Civil Liberties Association
90 Eglinton Avenue, Suite 900
Toronto, ON M4P 2Y3
(416) 363-0321
Website: https://ccla.org
Facebook and Twitter: @cancivlib
The Canadian Civil Liberties Association is dedicated
  to protecting the civil liberties of Canadians. One
  of its focus areas is protecting citizens and others
  in the realms of online expression and the personal
  privacy concerns of marginalized groups.

Center for Democracy and Technology
1401 K Street NW, Suite 200
Washington, DC 20005
(202) 637-9800

Email: press@cdt.org
Facebook and Twitter: @CenDemTech
The Center for Democracy and Technology is a non-profit that fights for privacy rights online, including against government intrusions.

Digital Responsibility Organization
3561 Homestead Road, #113
Santa Clara, CA 95051-5161
Email: info@digitalresponsibility.org
Website: http://www.digitalresponsibility.org
Digital Responsibility helps people take control of their online lives through articles, events, and news. It also offers scholarships to high school, college, and graduate school students.

Electronic Frontier Foundation (EFF)
815 Eddy Street
San Francisco, CA 94109
(415) 436-9333
Facebook and Twitter: @EFF
The EFF specializes in legally representing people for their rights in cyberspace. It fights to protect online speech and against online government surveillance.

Office of the Priavcy Commissioner of Canada
30 Victoria Street
Gatineau, QC K1A 1H3
Canada
(819) 994-5444
Website: https://www.priv.gc.ca

Facebook: @ PrivCanada

Twitter: @ PrivacyPrivee

The Office of the Privacy Commissioner (OPC) of
Canada is a Canadian federal government office
dedicated to protecting and promoting the privacy
rights of individuals, especially when it comes to
their interactions with the government, and also with
private parties, such as corporations.

Reputation Management

333 West Washington Street, Suite 140

Syracuse, NY 13202

(888) 613-8496

Email: info@reputationmanagement.com

Website: https://www.reputationmanagement.com

Twitter: @repmgmt_com

Facebook: @reputationmanagementcom

This company is run by reputation management experts
who give advice and guidance for anyone who needs
to protect or repair his or her online reputation.

FOR FURTHER READING

Abramovitz, Melissa. *Online Predators*. (Digital Issues). San Diego, CA: Referencepoint Press, 2016.

Bryan, Dale-Marie. *Smartphone Safety and Privacy*. New York, NY: Rosen Publishing, 2014.

Cunningham, Anne. *Privacy and Security in the Digital Age*. Farmington Hills, MI: Greenhaven Publishing, 2017.

Furgang, Kathy. *Internet Surveillance and How to Protect Your Privacy*. New York, NY: Rosen Publishing, 2017.

January, Brendan. *Information Insecurity: Privacy Under Siege*. Minneapolis, MN: Twenty-First Century Books, 2015.

Parks, Peggy. *Online Privacy*. San Diego, CA: Referencepoint Press, 2016.

Sadleir, Emma. *Selfies, Sexts, and Smartphones: A Teenager's Online Survival Guide*. New York, NY: Penguin Books, 2017.

Stuckey, Rachel. *Digital Dangers*. New York, NY: Crabtree Publishing, 2015.

Suen, Anastasia. *Online Privacy and the Law*. New York, NY: Rosen Publishing, 2013.

Wilkinson, Colin. *Everything You Need to Know about Digital Privacy*. New York, NY: Rosen Publishing, 2017.

BIBLIOGRAPHY

Bartiromo, Michael. "How to Get Your Embarrassing Photos Off the Internet." Fox News, October 23, 2012. http://www.foxnews.com/lifestyle/2012/10/23/how-to-get-your-embarrassing-photos-off-internet.html.

CareerBuilder. "Number of Employers Using Social Media to Screen Candidates Has Increased 500 Percent over the Last Decade." April 28, 2016. https://www.careerbuilder.com/share/aboutus/pressreleasesdetail.aspx?ed=12%2F31%2F2016&id=pr945&sd=4%2F28%2F2016.

Coffman, Leanne. Email interview with the author. April 12, 2018.

Curran, Dylan. "Are You Ready? Here Is All the Data Facebook and Google Have on You." *Guardian,* March 30, 2018. https://www.theguardian.com/commentisfree/2018/mar/28/all-the-data-facebook-google-has-on-you-privacy.

Dachis, Adam. "How to Fix Internet Embarrassments and Improve Your Reputation Online." Lifehacker, October 17, 2011. https://lifehacker.com/5850288/how-to-fix-internet-embarrassments-and-improve-your-online-reputation.

Grant, Christopher. Email interview with the author. April 14, 2018.

Hosselet, Alex. "When It Comes to Posting Photos on Social Media, Teens Are Anything but Spontaneous, New Study Shows." Media Smarts/Cision, April 19,

2017. https://www.newswire.ca/news-releases /when-it-comes-to-posting-photos-on-social-media -teens-are-anything-but-spontaneous-new-study -shows-619814683.html.

MacBlane, Brianna. "Reputation Management 101: How to Remove Negative Search Results." Reputation Management, December 15, 2017. https://www .reputationmanagement.com/blog/reputation -management-101-how-to-remove-negative-search -results.

Meyer, Thomas. Email interview with the author. April 16, 2018.

Naughton, John. "Internet Security: 10 Ways to Keep Your Personal Data Safe from Online Snoopers." *Guardian*, September 16, 2013. https://www .theguardian.com/technology/2013 /sep/16/10-ways-keep-personal-data-safe.

Orr, Nicole. Personal interview with the author. April 17, 2018.

Pannon, Alexandra. "How to Teach Teens about Cybersecurity." *US News and World Report*, October 12, 2015. https://www.usnews.com /education/blogs/high-school-notes/2015/10/12 /how-to-teach-teens-about-cybersecurity.

Purewal, Sarah Jacobsson. "5 Tips for Finding Anything, about Anyone, Online." C/Net, January 22, 2015. https://www.cnet.com/how-to/5-tips-for-find ing-anything-about-anyone-online.

R., Leon. Email interview with the author. April 13, 2018.

Ricker, Susan. "What You Miss Out on When Your Social Media Profiles are Invisible to Employers."

CareerBuilder, October 27, 2014. https://www
.careerbuilder.com/advice/what-you-miss-out-on
-when-your-social-media-profiles-are-invisible-to
-employers.

Rubenking, Neil. "The Best Antivirus Protection of
2018." *PC Mag,* April 14, 2018. https://www.pcmag
.com/article2/0,2817,2372364,00.asp.

Sherr, Ian. "Hard Question: Q&A with Mark Zuckerberg
on Protecting People's Information." Facebook
Newsroom, April 4, 2018. https://newsroom.fb.com
/news/2018/04
/hard-questions-protecting-peoples-information.

Soltan, Liz. "Sharing Inappropriate Photos or
Information Online." Digital Responsibility.org.
Retrieved March 25, 2018. http://www
.digitalresponsibility.org
/sharing-inappropriate-photos-or-information-online.

UC Irvine. "Teens Post Online Content to Appear
Interesting, Popular, and Attractive." *Science Daily
News,* February 16, 2018. https://www.sciencedaily
.com/releases/2018/02/180216113910.htm.

Weisbaum, Herb. "Identity Fraud Hits Record Number
of Americans in 2016." NBC News, February 2,
2017. https://www.nbcnews.com/business
/consumer/identity-fraud-hits-record-number
-americans-2016-n715756.

Zuckerberg, Mark. Facebook post. March 21, 2018.
https://www.facebook.com/zuck
/posts/10104712037900071.

INDEX

A

anonymity, 26
  Muttr, 26
  Secret, 26
  Vent, 26
  Whisper, 26
  Yik Yak, 26
antivirus software, 46, 53, 54, 56
  features, 56
  McAfee Antivirus Plus, 58
  Symantec Norton Antivirus
    Basic, 58
  Webroot SecureAnywhere
    Antivirus, 58
authentication, 53, 59
awareness, 7–8, 9

B

Berkman Center for Internet
  Society, 4
Bing, 35

C

Cambridge Analytica, 34, 55
CareerBuilder, 22, 28
  Haefner, Rosemary, 22
college admissions, 4, 5, 22
Connect Safely, 16
controversial topics, 22

credit report, 50
Curran, Dylan, 32, 33
cyberbullying, 38, 39
  suicide, 39
  types, 38–39
Cyberbullying Research
  Center, 14

D

Data Privacy Day, 9
  annual theme, 9
Digital Millennium Copyright
  Act (DCMA), 36
digital nomads, 7, 8–9
digital privacy, 5, 6, 9, 12, 14,
  15, 16, 38, 49, 53, 55, 63
  breaches, 55
  respecting, 9
  settings, 14, 16
  who it affects, 12
digital security, 7, 8, 9, 18, 48,
  60, 63
  apps, 8
  for companies, 60, 61
  penetration testing, 48, 49
  programs, 8
discriminatory comments, 24
DuckDuckGo, 35

E

electronic hive mind, 12

email authentication, 17–18
enabling trust, 9
Equifax, 55

F

Facebook, 11, 14, 22, 32, 34,
   49, 55
   user data collection, 32, 34
   what it knows, 32
Federal Trade Commission
   (FTC), 50, 52

G

Google, 29–30, 32, 33, 36
   email, 30, 32
   location tracking, 29, 32
   searches, 29, 30
   user information, 32
   what it knows, 29–30, 32
Grant, Christopher, 11–12

H

habit, 4

I

identity theft, 5, 11, 12, 40, 41,
   43, 44, 48, 50–52
   cell phone accounts, 44, 45
   credit score, 5, 41
   Fair Credit Billing Act, 50
   fraud, 43
   pitfalls of, 5, 41, 43

reporting, 50, 52

J

Javelin Strategy and Research,
   41, 43
   Pascual, Al, 43

M

Meyer, Thomas, 15

N

National Cyber Security
   Alliance, 9, 18
   Kaiser, Michael, 18
   Naughton, John, 61, 63

O

online permanence, 6, 15, 39, 49
online profile, 33
   search, 33, 34–36
Orr, Nicole, 7, 8, 9

P

password managers, 14, 46,
   53, 59, 61
   Dashlane, 14
   LastPass, 14, 61
   1Password, 61
   SplashID, 14
password protection, 46, 61
   facial recognition, 61

fingerprint ID, 61
iris scanning, 61
simple, 61
passwords, 12–13, 14, 45, 46, 59
  changing, 14, 50
  creating, 13, 59
  sharing, 14
  storing, 14, 46, 47–48
PayPal, 45, 46
PC Mag, 54, 56
peer approval, 19, 21
Pew Research Center, 4
photos, 21, 32, 35, 36
potential employers, 22, 24, 28
  positive examples for, 24
  recruiters, 24
precedents, 15
Privacy Rights Clearinghouse, 55
  Givens, Beth, 55

R

red flags for potential employers, 22, 24
  complaining, 24
  controversial topics, 22
  discriminatory comments, 24
  sexual posts, 24
reputation, 4
Reputation Management, 39

S

safeguarding data, 9

safety rules, 45–47
Safety Training Solution, 60
  Coffman, Leanne, 60, 61
scams, 12
security software, 17, 46, 53
  Avast, 17
  AVG, 17
  Avira, 17
  Bitdefender, 17
  Kaspersky, 17
selfies, 21
social media, 4, 6, 11, 14, 15, 16, 17, 19, 22, 25, 28, 38
  factors to consider, 6, 14, 23
  friends, 17
  motivations, 19, 21, 38
  privacy settings, 14, 16–17
  profiles, 28
social networking, 6, 22
Social Security number, 44, 47, 50–51
Soltan, Liz, 24
statistics, 4, 22
surveillance, 33

T

taking precautions, 4–5, 8–9, 11, 12, 13, 17–18, 23, 46–48, 49, 53
  pen and paper, 26
Tallim, Jane, 21–22
Terach, Joseph, 24, 28
Twitter, 14, 22

U

University of California, Irvine, 19

V

venting, 26

W

Wi-Fi, 61
WWGS rule, 23

Y

Yahoo, 35, 55
Yau, Joanna, 19, 21
YouTube, 30, 32

Z

Zuckerberg, Mark, 34, 55

ABOUT THE AUTHOR

Tamra Orr is the author of numerous educational books for readers of all ages. She graduated from Ball State University in Indiana and currently lives in the Pacific Northwest with her family. There she loves to go camping, read tons of books, write lots of letters, and spend far too much time on the internet. She is just old enough that her kids teach her about digital privacy instead of the other way around.

PHOTO CREDITS